W9-CLC-392

NO LONGER PROPERTY
OF HAWORTH
MUNICIPAL LIBRARY

CHARLESTON
PUBLISHERS

HEROES OF
RACING

# JIMMIE JOHNSON
## *Racing Champ*

### by Marty Gitlin

Haworth Municipal Library
OF Haworth Avenue
MUNICIPAL LIBRARY
Haworth, NJ 07641
201-384-Avenue
LIBRARY

**Enslow Publishers, Inc.**
40 Industrial Road
Box 398
Berkeley Heights, NJ 07922
USA
http://www.enslow.com

Copyright © 2008 by Enslow Publishers, Inc.

All rights reserved.

No part of this book may be reproduced by any means without the written permission of the publisher.

**Library of Congress Cataloging-in-Publication Data**
Gitlin, Marty.
    Jimmie Johnson : racing champ / Marty Gitlin.
        p. cm. — (Heroes of racing)
    Includes bibliographical references and index.
    Summary: "A biography of NASCAR sports star Jimmie Johnson"—Provided by publisher.
    ISBN-13: 978-0-7660-2999-6
    ISBN-10: 0-7660-2999-9
    1.  Johnson, Jimmie, 1975—Juvenile literature. 2.  Automobile racing drivers—United States—Biography—Juvenile literature.  I. Title.
    GV1032.J54G58 2008
    796.72092—dc22
    [B]
                                                    2007016074

**Credits**
Editorial Direction: Red Line Editorial (Bob Temple)
Editor: Sue Green
Designer: Becky Daum

Printed in the United States of America

10 9 8 7 6 5 4 3 2 1

**To Our Readers:** We have done our best to make sure all Internet addresses in this book were active and appropriate when we went to press. However, the author and the publisher have no control over and assume no liability for the material available on those Internet sites or on other Web sites they may link to. Any comments or suggestions can be sent by e-mail to comments@enslow.com or to the address on the back cover.

**Disclaimer:** This publication is not affiliated with, endorsed by, or sponsored by NASCAR. NASCAR®, WINSTON CUP®, NEXTEL CUP, BUSCH SERIES and CRAFTSMAN TRUCK SERIES are trademarks owned or controlled by the National Association for Stock Car Auto Racing, Inc., and are registered where indicated.

**Photo credits:** Robert E. Klein/AP Images, 1, 39; Mark J. Terrill/AP Images, 4; Ric Feld/AP Images, 6, 70; Terry Renna/AP Images, 12, 92; Chuck Burton/AP Images, 16, 41, 46, 113; David Maung/AP Images, 24; Stuart Ramson/AP Images, 29; Frank Polich/AP Images, 36; Henry Durand/AP Images, 51; Mike McCarn/AP Images, 58-59; John Harrell/AP Images, 61; John Harrelson/AP Images, 68; The Charlotte Observer, Chris Keane/AP Images, 71; Greg Suvino/AP Images, 74; Daytona Beach News-Journal, Nigel Cook/AP Images, 82; Don Petersen/AP Images, 85; J. Pat Carter/AP Images, 90-91; Tom Strattman/AP Images, 94; Gerry Broome/AP Images, 96-97; Wilfredo Lee/AP Images, 105, 107; Dave Parker/AP Images, 108-109

**Cover Photo:** Robert E. Klein/AP Images

# CONTENTS

**W**inning did not matter when Jimmie Johnson was a kid—not to his parents and not so much to himself.

But it mattered now. It mattered when his critics claimed greatness would always elude him. It mattered when he was showered with questions from the media about why he had never won a NASCAR championship. It mattered when he could not eliminate his own self-doubts until he earned a title.

**Jimmie Johnson, in the Lowe's car, and Tony Stewart battle for the lead down the backstretch in the 2005 Sony HD 500.**

It mattered on November 19, 2006, when sixteen laps into the Ford 400, blood ran down the right side of his nose, courtesy of a spring that had fallen off the car of Kurt Busch. Yet Johnson continued to speed around the track.

On that day, in that race, thirty-one-year-old Jimmie Johnson was going to quiet those critics, silence the media, and eliminate that self-doubt. No,

**Johnson prepares for practice for the Bass Pro Shops MBNA 500 in Georgia on October 28, 2005.**

he did not win the Ford 400. He did not need to. He finished ninth, and that clinched his first Nextel Cup crown.

## A CHAMPIONSHIP SEASON

Johnson had been among the most consistently strong NASCAR drivers since his first full season in 2002. Yet there always proved to be some

**Though Johnson clinched the 2006 Nextel Cup title in the season-ending Ford 400, Greg Biffle won that event for the third consecutive year.**

**DID YOU KNOW?**

stretch that became an enemy year after year. Just a year earlier he had entered the final week in second place overall, but a blown tire knocked him out of the Ford 400 and dropped him to fifth.

That race caused a rift between Johnson and crew chief Chad Knaus. The driver wanted to pull in for a pit stop with a punctured right-rear tire. Knaus told him to keep racing. Some even speculated that the two would part ways. It took a meeting with car owner Rick Hendrick to smooth out the situation.

Nothing like that was going to happen with the title on the line in 2006. It just could not happen again. Johnson made certain of it on that fall day in Homestead, Florida.

But, as luck would have it, Johnson had fallen to fortieth place after his pit stop to repair the damage

## YOUNG LEADER
At just fourteen years old, Chad Knaus served as his father's crew chief at Rockford Speedway, near their Illinois home.

to his nose. He had to finish at least twelfth to snare the championship.

"That's our drama for the day," Knaus said on the radio to his driver. "Now you've got to pass all those cars."

In years past, Johnson might have been overwhelmed—but not in 2006.

"10-4," he replied confidently.[1]

Johnson began zipping past the competition. It took him sixty laps to gain the necessary twenty-nine spots. Matt Kenseth, who rested in second place in the overall points standings, could not catch him even if he had won the race.

Three hours later, it was done. Not only had Johnson finally captured the Nextel Cup crown, but he became the first driver in NASCAR history to win the Daytona 500, Brickyard 400, and overall title in the same year.

Now he knew how all the past champions felt. Now he knew the joy highly successful Hendrick

Motorsports teammates such as Jeff Gordon experienced when they clinched NASCAR titles.

"It may take a while to sink in," said a giddy Johnson after the race. "I knew we had a great team. I knew all along we could do it. We just had some bad luck at the start of the Chase. And then we got some momentum, and some guys had some bad luck, to let us get back into it. This is everything I've ever wanted, to be a champion."[2]

## A ROUGH PATCH

It did not appear seven weeks earlier that Johnson would compete for the 2006 championship, let alone win it. An accident at Talladega knocked him back to twenty-fourth place in that event and maintained his position in eighth place in the points standings. It also compounded a horrible stretch that had sent him reeling.

Johnson had been in first place nearly the entire season before a run of nine consecutive races in which he placed tenth or lower. A wreck in New Hampshire resulted in a thirty-ninth-place finish in that race and plummeted Johnson from second to ninth overall. He took no higher than thirteenth in the next three weeks. With six events remaining, he sat in seventh place.

It seemed a certainty the title that had escaped his grasp the last five years was going to elude him again. In fact, the possibility existed that he would complete the season lower than he ever had. After all, he had never finished lower than fifth overall, even as a rookie. Though he had established himself as a comeback driver, especially when fall approached, most believed he had fallen too far back to win.

But something strange happened. Unlike in seasons past, Johnson did not worry. He kept calm, just like he did in his days racing as a teenager in El Cajon, California. He rediscovered the laid-back attitude instilled in him by parents who did not believe winning was everything. He was not putting pressure on himself.

"I really haven't been worrying about things that worried me before," Johnson said during the tough 2006 run. "The things that made me lose sleep at night the past few years aren't there. I have a smile on my face."[3]

That smile would soon become wider. Johnson finished the 2006 season on an unprecedented blitz to leap back into the championship hunt. He jumped to third by winning the Subway 500, inched into second by taking second the following week in Atlanta, then vaulted back into first by placing second in Texas. A third consecutive second-place performance the next Sunday in Phoenix set up his title clinching at the Ford 400.

## FACING CRITICISM

Johnson had quieted the critics. Poor stretches had always doomed him, but not this year. In 2005, a mid-season slump sent him reeling. In 2004, nine finishes of tenth or lower during a ten-race stretch ruined his title hopes. In 2002 and 2003, inconsistency through late summer killed his chances.

So Johnson understood the skepticism. He did not enjoy hearing about it, but he could not argue that it was not justified. In fact, the criticism he received for failing to win a championship at least meant folks inside and outside the racing world believed he was capable of achieving that goal.

"We look at it as a compliment to hear that because people expect a lot out of us," Johnson said after winning the 2006 crown. "Don't get me wrong, we didn't want to miss an opportunity when we were in great position to try to become a champion. But we haven't felt that burden and pressure.

**DID YOU KNOW?** By the end of the 2007 season, Johnson had averaged more victories per season (5.5) than any other active driver.

"I'm not saying we would have been happy if we didn't win the championship, but in a couple of days we can look back and be very proud of what we've done. Now that title can't linger around any longer."[4]

**Rick Hendrick, Johnson, and Darian Grubb celebrate a win.**

Perhaps Johnson should have known something would be different in 2006 when he opened with a victory in the prestigious Daytona 500. He had placed no lower than fifth at Daytona since 2003, but starting the season with a win meant a great deal.

Johnson placed second in California the following week and won the third race of the season in Las Vegas. He was solidly atop the points standings and would remain there into late August.

## CHANGING HIS OUTLOOK

Even though he experienced a prolonged slump in September and early October, he was not going to be denied. A difference not only in attitude but in philosophy played a critical role in Johnson's success.

He knew he had to throw strategy out the window. Only a go-for-broke approach could win the championship after he had fallen so far behind. He was no longer going to concern himself with the competition. After all, that was beyond his control. He would race aggressively.

But if he were to win, every member of his team had to maximize his performance. Knaus was exhausted. He realized he was not on top of his game, so he began to delegate more responsibility.

**DID YOU KNOW?**

The DirecTV 500 was the only race in which Johnson earned the pole position, yet he won five events in 2006.

"I'm making a lot of the staff back at the shop work a little harder than they have in the past," Knaus said. "I tried to bear all of the responsibility, and that's not something you can do. That's one thing that we did this year, to spread the load a little more across the guys and make them a little bit more responsible for what they've got to do. It's definitely paid dividends."[5]

There could be no greater dividend for Johnson than his first Nextel Cup championship. And after that exciting, emotional day, he planned a calm dinner in downtown Miami with his wife, Chandra.

It would be a satisfying night. Johnson had finally accomplished the ultimate goal. He could reflect on the season and on a career in which capturing a title had always been the driving force—even if his parents did not care about winning.

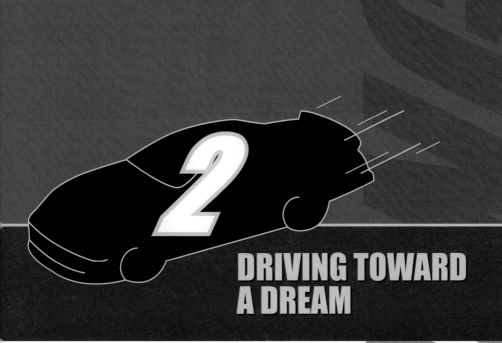

# DRIVING TOWARD
# A DREAM

In 1971, a baby was born in California. He would eventually break the mold by becoming a NASCAR phenomenon raised on the West Coast while most of the stars on that circuit were deeply rooted in the South.

That baby was Jeff Gordon, who went on to win four Winston Cup championships.

Four years later, another baby was born in California who would also take the racing world by storm. That baby was Jimmie Johnson. The day was September 17, 1975.

**Jimmie Johnson (right) watches his brother Jessie race with his brother Jarit (left) and other family members.**

Jimmie was born in the town of El Cajon. His father, Gary, and mother, Cathy, shared with their son an interest in racing. By the time Jimmie was four years old, he was scooting around the California deserts on a "pee wee" motorcycle that could travel no faster than 5 miles per hour (8 kilometers per hour).

That was nothing special. Many children in California enjoy such activities, even before they attend kindergarten.

There was one difference, however. Even at that young age, Jimmie found racing created a spark inside of him. That spark remains with him to this day. He and his family, which includes brothers Jessie (also a driver) and Jarit, spent a great deal of time taking Jimmie and his motorcycle to tracks throughout California and other areas of the southwest United States.

## SUPPORT FROM HOME

Gary had the background to provide his son with expert advice. He was a mechanic on a desert buggy and was interested in various forms of racing. That love of the sport quickly rubbed off on Jimmie, who thoroughly enjoyed the thrill of competition.

### THREE OF A KIND
**Jarit and Jessie appeared with their brother Jimmie Johnson in a Levi Strauss advertising campaign.**

But Jimmie's parents were unlike those who pushed their children into a hobby or even a career for the sake of their own egos. In fact, they encouraged Jimmie to compete for the love of racing, not to fill up the trophy case in their El Cajon home. Their goal was to not only instill in him a passion for a particular activity, but to strengthen his work ethic.

The philosophy paid off. Jimmie experienced tremendous competitive success at an early age, even winning a class championship at the age of eight. But it would not have been possible had he not been a student of the sport and developed a love for it. Most of all, it had to be enjoyable.

"If I ended up never getting (to be a NASCAR star), they still would have been very proud of me and happy with what I tried to do," Jimmie said of his family. "That's the thing with my parents . . . they just want to see you work hard and where you land is cool. It's all about working hard.

"I'd watch these parents who would force their kids to win, force them to jump the big doubles, force them to do all this stuff, and my dad would be over there leaning up against a tree whistling at us as we went by. If we got off the bike and we'd tried as hard as we could, he was fine. It didn't matter where we finished. That's something I've been extremely lucky about—that my parents took that approach with us."[1]

## MOVING UP

Gary helped his son every step of the way. When Jimmie was fifteen, his father arranged a tryout for him with the five-buggy Superlite team on the Mickey Thompson Stadium Off-Road Series, which was growing in popularity. Gary began working for BF Goodrich as a truck driver around that same time, so he asked company representative Dan Newsome for help.

Newsome pulled a few strings. Soon Jimmie became the youngest driver in the history of the

Mickey Thompson Entertainment Group. He performed so well that season that he landed a spot in the Chevrolet-backed Grand National Truck division the following year.

> ## FEELING THE HEAT
> During his youth, Johnson raced in the desert in temperatures often exceeding 100 degrees Fahrenheit (38 degrees Celsius).

That soon became a pattern. Jimmie would move up a rung on the ladder, dominate, and then rise to the next level.

By the time he was ready to earn his regular driver's license, Jimmie was making a name for himself in the tough Grand National Truck division. He caught the attention of Herb Fishel, who was head of worldwide racing for Chevrolet. Among Fishel's duties was spotting talented young drivers. He liked what he saw of the California teenager.

"A lot of people know Herb for keeping an eye out for young drivers," Jimmie said. "He expressed an interest in me when I was 16, and he's so deep into motorsports (that) he knows what's happening at all times and he has my best interests at heart. With my background and upbringing, there have been a few people that made this possible, and Herb's one of them."[2]

**THEY SAID IT**

"Dirt racing was everything to me as a kid growing up; and I'd see those NASCAR races on TV and I didn't think it was possible for me to get there."

**– Jimmie Johnson**

The relationship with Fishel translated into a Chevrolet truck for Jimmie to race in the stadium series. It also helped Jimmie to grow in other ways. Fishel provided training in public speaking and public relations that would allow him to handle the environment both outside and inside the track. He worked as hard tackling those lessons as he did developing into one of the most promising young drivers in the country.

## A COMPETITIVE SPIRIT

None of that would have mattered, however, had Jimmie failed to take advantage of his talent. But he certainly did capitalize on his opportunity, winning three straight Grand National Truck Series titles from 1992 to 1994. He also captured the Short-Course Off-Road Enthusiasts Desert championship in 1994.

When Jimmie began racing in the national truck series, he knew some people thought of him as nothing but a novelty act. After all, he was only sixteen years old. Though raised by his parents to value the enjoyment of racing more than winning, his natural competitive spirit began to surface.

That was one motivating factor for him. Another was his desire to work his way up the ladder until he was at the highest level of NASCAR racing.

"They started testing me for the ride, and I got in," Jimmie said about his first experience with the Grand National Truck Series. "When I got involved with Chevrolet, they were interested in looking at and building a future, and I think Herb Fishel probably set that up the most. He's the one who presented me to Chevrolet. He really got the ball rolling at Chevrolet and had a lot of interest in me. I expressed to them where I wanted to go with my racing, and that was stock cars."[3]

Jimmie understood that he could pursue that dream, but he was several years away from making it a reality. In the meantime, he needed to hone his skills in the Stadium Off-Road series.

It was during those three years that Jimmie began developing his own driving style and strategies. When he began racing trucks, he was too careless. He battered his trucks, which led him to worry that he would not continue to receive the opportunity to drive. Jimmie decided he had to become less reckless while maintaining his aggressive approach.

"When I got into stadium trucks, I tore up plenty of equipment and drove (team owner) Jon Nelson crazy," Jimmie said. "But I learned some hard lessons through that. At the same time, I had to go out there and be fast and show that I have the potential and can win races. So I've been able to adapt to a certain style: to push when I need to race hard, but at the same time not take unnecessary risks."[4]

Throughout their son's three-year stint as a Grand National Truck driver, Jimmie's parents made it clear he needed to perform well in school. In fact, they set the bar at a "B" average. Anything lower and he would no longer be allowed to race.

That was no problem for Jimmie. The work ethic Gary and Cathy instilled in him made it easy for him to keep up with his studies and still concentrate on his goal while driving. That goal was to earn a spot on the Winston Cup circuit. He considered its drivers to be the premier auto racers in the world.

With every season at every level, Jimmie showed he was getting closer to achieving his dream.

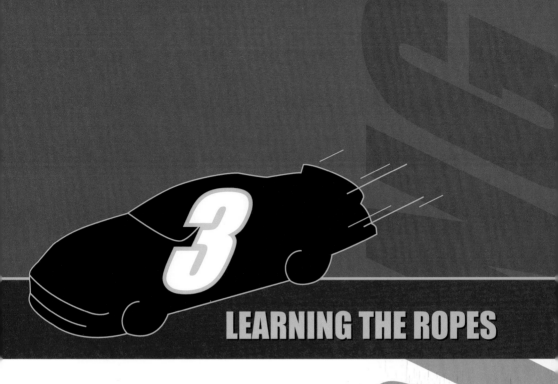

The learning process is sometimes slow. Jimmie Johnson vowed when he began racing trucks in the early 1990s that he was going to temper his aggressive style with a cautious approach. He knew at an early point in his career that the folks who shell out millions of dollars for trucks and other vehicles get a bit upset when the drivers they employ batter their investments.

That determination helped Johnson win three consecutive Grand National Truck series championships against mostly older competition. But

**A trophy truck flies through the air at a high point in the road during the Baja 1000 race near Ojos Negros, Mexico.**

one incident in the Baja 1000 during the mid-1990s shocked him back into understanding that disaster can happen in an instant.

"I took down the 880-mile marker when I crashed," Johnson recalled. "I thought I could drive straight through. I was leading the race, and I had a problem, threw the power steering belt and the oil pump belt off the truck. Then when we tried to start the truck, the starter motor was dead. We lost about an hour or so trying to get the truck back on the road.

"We got it back on the road, and at that point I figured I was out of the race, but I was still charging hard. Little did I know that the other two trucks that had passed me had broken down, which put me back in the lead. So I'm charging hard. I'd been driving for 20 hours then (and) hadn't slept yet. So I dozed off a little bit. I drive into a rainstorm that woke me up, and I was still on the track, but I was coming up on a turn.

"I was going way too fast for the turn. I tried to slow down, but I knew I was going off the road, so I figured I better go off straight. When I plowed through everything, there was a rock the size of a Volkswagen Bug sitting there. I hit the rock and flipped and flipped. I'm down at the bottom of this little sand wash.

"You wouldn't believe this, but there were about 100 Mexicans at the bottom of this wash, with bonfires and their wives and everything, watching the race. A lot of times the people who watch the race like that go out and pull markers down and wait to see a crash. Well, they got to see their crash.

**DID YOU KNOW?**

Among other racing superstars who spent time racing in the desert were Indianapolis 500 winners Rick Mears and Parnelli Jones.

"I spent two days with those guys until the communication went to my crew guys.

My chase truck had a problem and was broken down. By the time the chase truck for my teammate, Larry Raglund, got to me, it was almost two days later."[1]

## LEARNING LESSONS

Johnson learned a lesson in that race that has remained with him ever since. Aggressiveness without a sense of caution can be dangerous.

"I had a lot of time to sit there and reflect," said Johnson about the hours spent after the accident. "I drove for John Nelson, and John always wanted you to run hard. He really pushed me to charge hard in the stadium stuff.

"I was 18 years old, would get up ready to charge hard, and I got into a desert truck. You really have to have some experience to race those. You race against the clock; it's an endurance race. After that crash, I really started reflecting on my style. Since that crash—and I raced two more years of off-road—I never had that truck upside-down, and I've never torn anything up in stock cars.

"Ever since then, I've been on the right side of the aggressive line, where before I crossed it quite frequently and had been lucky enough to save it. But I think I've gotten a little older and a little more mature. I still feel I'm pretty aggressive."[2]

No setback could knock Johnson off the road to stardom. He not only won Rookie of the Year honors in the Grand National Truck series, he also earned that award in Short-Course Off-Road Drivers' Association (SODA) Winter Series and American Speed Association (ASA) competitions.

During his short stint on the SODA circuit, Johnson also began to show the off-track talents provided to him by Herb Fishel. He proved articulate and poised enough to work as a commentator on broadcasts for sports cable network ESPN. Just barely past his teenage years, Johnson was displaying a versatility and work ethic that made his parents proud.

His success as a driver made them proud as well. Johnson won the SODA championship in 1996 and 1997.

Off-road driving, however, is not the ideal training ground for stock car racing. The world of differences had him yearning to take his career to the next level.

## PREPARING FOR THE FUTURE

Johnson preferred stadium to desert racing. Competing in trucks on huge expanses of sand simply does not prepare drivers for the heavy traffic and tight turns found in stock car competitions.

"The stadium racing I did is sort of like road course racing where you could set somebody up and you'd have a strong section of the track to pass them,"

# CREDIT WHERE CREDIT IS DUE
Among those Johnson credits for his style
of racing is former Supercross champion
and ASA teammate Rick Johnson.

Johnson said. "In stock cars, you're always turning left, and it's really the same at either end. Learning how to pass in a stock car was difficult, but as far as running in traffic, I was used to that from my stadium experience.

"That's one thing I didn't quite care much for, racing in the desert. You'd chase somebody's dust cloud, bust through it, tap him once or twice, he'd move over, and you'd go on. You never really raced anybody for anything. That's part of what my problem was in the desert, too. I'd chase all the dust clouds and wouldn't drive my own race."[3]

Even if Johnson did drive his own race, he was never driving just for himself. Like all competitors in his sport, he was driving for his owners and team members.

Fishel, along with fellow off-road team owners Stan and Randy Herzog, understood that Johnson had achieved all there was to achieve up to that point. They helped him break into stock car racing at a relatively high level.

**Johnson and his wife, Chandra, pose during red carpet arrivals at the world premiere of the film "Invincible" on August 23, 2006.**

**THEY SAID IT**

"Every track and track surface has its own rhythm, and asphalt is all about rhythm."

— Jimmie Johnson on his move from dirt tracks to asphalt

In 1998, Johnson would compete in the short-track series of the American Speed Association (ASA). His name would be forever linked with world champions of auto racing who sped through that circuit on the road to greatness. Brilliant drivers such as Alan Kulwicki, Darrell Waltrip, Rusty Wallace, and Mark Martin had all raced in that series.

Both his professional and personal lives were growing at the same time. Johnson had met model Jessica Bergendahl at a Christmas party during his off-road racing career. She finally agreed to a date with him nine months later. The couple remained together for several years.

"Jessica is a beautiful blonde-haired California girl just like you would imagine," Johnson said. "She baby-sits me with genuine support and love. She's never tried to slow me down from what I want to do. Someday I'll get married. It's important to have that stability in my life."[4]

Johnson did not marry Jessica, though he did marry his wife, Chandra, in 2004. Just like other men his age, Johnson began thinking more about his personal life. But he knew a successful career in auto racing could translate into a far more rewarding existence off the track.

He actually ran three stock car races in 1997, then placed fourth overall in the ASA short-track series in 1998. It was his first experience performing on asphalt. On-track racing forced him to maintain a level of concentration that had not been necessary in his previous driving experiences. Handling trucks in a short-sprint series was a far cry from handling stock cars at blazing speeds for several hundred miles.

"It's really a lot different inside the car, training your brain to be alert for 250 laps," Johnson said. "When I ran the desert series, you raced against the clock for 20 hours. The majority of the racing I've done in the stadium series has been 15-minute sprint races, and those

## GAINING NATIONAL ATTENTION

Johnson received his first major TV exposure as an ASA rookie in 1998. Every race was televised by a national cable network despite the fact that nearly all of them were held in the Midwest.

were the long ones. So to go 300 or 400 laps at a whack was something I had to train myself to do.

"After a pit stop, even if it was the first one, I'd be thinking the race was almost over, even if we had three or four more (stops) to go. Being able to save the equipment, knowing that this might be the last time putting left-side tires on, maybe I'll have another set of rights, and when you spin the left rear tire you're also spinning the rights—just learning about all that, it's been a pretty steep learning curve."[5]

That learning curve was the same for his fellow drivers. The difference is that Johnson grasped those lessons more successfully and often with greater passion than they did. He also had more talent.

The racing world was about to find that out in a hurry. Johnson was ready to climb another rung on the ladder to greatness.

# RISING TO THE TOP

Jimmie Johnson was no child when he crouched into the stock car for his NASCAR Busch series debut in 1998. And he was nearly twenty-four years old when he competed in his first 1999 event on Independence Day.

Others have begun their Busch careers at earlier ages, but most of them boasted far more experience racing on asphalt. Johnson had zipped around asphalt tracks only forty-three times during the course of two seasons before his first Busch event. The majority of his fellow drivers required several years of priming before taking on the circuit one step below the Winston Cup, now known as the Nextel Cup.

Not Johnson. He earned a promotion from the ASA in a hurry. And if any folks believed he was not ready, he erased their doubts at the Milwaukee Mile on that July 4.

Driving a Herzog Chevrolet, Johnson finished a strong seventh. He had performed well twice at that track before, but that was in ASA events. Few thought he could race with the best Busch had to offer with so little experience.

That was to define Johnson throughout his career, during which he has always risen to and even beyond the level of his competition. He had yet to begin proving himself as the most consistently strong driver on the NASCAR circuit, but that would not take long.

In fact, the better the competition, the better he performed.

## LEARNING THE ROPES

Johnson did not exactly tear up the Busch Series tracks, finishing tenth overall in 2000, which was his first full season on that circuit, and

**THEY SAID IT**

"There isn't anything that gets a driver ready for Busch Grand National racing besides Busch Grand National racing. ARCA, ASA, trucks, any of that stuff is just a totally different animal."

— Jimmie Johnson

eighth the following year. That success came despite the fact that he was racing mostly on tracks he had never experienced, so he did feel a high level of satisfaction.

By that time, Johnson had developed a strong relationship with crew chief Tony Liberati. The two worked out a system that allowed Johnson to get comfortable with each track every Friday, then work out the kinks before race day. The team did well enough to register six top-ten finishes in 2000 and nine more in 2001.

**DID YOU KNOW?**

Tony Liberati later experienced great success working with driver Todd Bodine in Busch Series competition.

Johnson's only taste of victory in the Busch Series was at the new Chicagoland Speedway in 2001, but he did add four top-five performances. He had failed to place that high in any race in 2000. He was improving slowly but surely. Johnson understood that taking NASCAR by storm in his first full Busch season was unrealistic.

Perhaps it was his parents' philosophy that hard work is more important than winning that allowed Johnson to remain patient. It served him well. He was able to stay focused and motivated while not losing his confidence.

"If I had been told when I left ASA that I would finish 10th in points the first year in Busch and

Johnson shows off his trophy after winning a 2001 race in Illinois.

in the second season win a race and finish in the top 10 again, I'd have said 'Shoot, I'll take that,'" Johnson said. "Winning the first race at Chicagoland was awesome. We didn't back into it. We raced hard. We were fortunate to hold off Ryan Newman at the end because he has been incredible in Penske equipment. I am so happy to get the first Busch win for the Herzogs, who have put a lot into me in six years, and for Tony."[1]

## GAINING UNEXPECTED ATTENTION

By that time, folks were starting to take notice. One of them was established NASCAR star Jeff Gordon, whose interest in him would change Johnson's life. Other drivers with as little experience and small number of triumphs in the Busch series do not get a second look from the big boys, but there was something about Johnson that interested Gordon.

In fact, there was something about Johnson that interested a number of Winston Cup owners. After his sponsor, Alltel, announced it was backing away in 2001, word got out that Johnson was going to be a "free agent" if another sponsor could not be found. Several Winston Cup owners, as well as Busch and truck series owners, expressed an interest.

Johnson was not surprised by the overtures from Busch and truck series owners. He was stunned, however, that Winston Cup owners felt he was ready.

Johnson believed that in order for Winston Cup owners to take him seriously, he needed to dominate in the Busch series. Johnson had been successful in the Busch series, but far from dominant. After all, he wasn't even a top-five driver in the Busch series yet. Johnson thought he still had a lot to learn. He couldn't imagine that the big boys would be interested in him yet.

**DID YOU KNOW?** Jimmie Johnson bettered Jeff Gordon in the Busch series race at Michigan Speedway in 2000, before which the two spoke about Johnson's Winston Cup future. Johnson finished sixth, one place ahead of Gordon, who was competing in Busch events in 2000 only as a promotion.

Finding a sponsor proved to be no problem. Herzog eventually landed headache relief medicine Excedrin to sponsor the 2001 car, but all the uncertainty and overtures from Winston Cup owners had overwhelmed Johnson. So he had a brainstorm. He decided to seek advice from Gordon. Little did he know that Gordon, whom he had never met, was interested in him as well.

Johnson felt nervous. He tried, but failed, to work up the nerve to approach Gordon. It would not be necessary, though. During the drivers meeting before the Busch race at the Michigan Speedway in 2000, he received a tap on the shoulder. It was Gordon, who was competing in several Busch races that year as a promotion.

The young driver spoke with Gordon after that meeting. He was planning to ask advice, but he did little talking.

Instead, all his questions and his dreams were answered when Gordon informed him that he and Hendrick Motorsports were interested in adding a fourth team, and they were considering Johnson to be the driver. It was not a sure thing. But Johnson left that meeting floating on Cloud 9.

"I can't describe my feelings when I walked out of that (meeting)," Johnson said. "I had gone in there confused, wondering, and searching for advice and had come out with the possibility of a ride with Jeff Gordon and Rick Hendrick.

**Johnson chats with Jeff Gordon (right) during practice.**

"I was simply trying to look ahead, be smart at a young age, and make sure I was going to have a ride in 2001. I wanted to stay with the Herzogs, but if anything happened to the team, I had to be prepared."[2]

Hendrick obviously felt the same as Gordon. After hearing of the conversation, he decided to pursue Johnson. Why? For the same reasons he signed the inexperienced Gordon nearly a decade earlier.

Hendrick saw similar potential in Johnson as he had with his four-time NASCAR champion.

The result was that Johnson signed a contract within the next month. Plans sped up to organize a new team with Johnson at the wheel in time for the 2002 season.

"The timing wasn't exactly right for us, but we were so impressed with Jimmie we needed to get to him before somebody else did," Hendrick said. "If you wait around when you see a guy who seems to have it all, the whole package, it's too late.

"It was much the same with signing Jeff (in 1992). We saw the talent first and then built around him. Jimmie is the reason we sped up this deal. He's very talented and sharp, his communication skills and feedback are incredible, and he's just a great individual.

"Chemistry has developed between him and Jeff over the past year, and I think what Jeff can offer as a teammate is a huge asset. Their driving styles are about the same. We're very fortunate to have Jimmie in the Hendrick stable. He's an excellent fit. I think

## INDY IDOL
Among Johnson's racing heroes while growing up was Indy Car driver Cale Yarborough, which is one reason Johnson did not consider stock car racing until his late teens.

**Johnson hugs car owner Rick Hendrick after winning the 2005 Coca-Cola 600.**

he's one of the best, if not the best, to come around in a long time."[3]

## MAKING A CHANGE

At the time, there were similarities and differences between Johnson and Gordon. Both hailed from

California. Both were clean-cut and handsome, which helped in terms of promotion and publicity. And despite their differences in experience, their ages were just four years apart.

But the biggest difference was that Gordon had won fifty-eight Winston Cup events. Johnson had not even raced in one.

Hendrick Motorsports was in the process of building an 85,000-square-foot (7,897-square-meter) facility at its complex. It planned on moving in both the Johnson and Gordon teams and training the younger driver on Winston Cup strategies and competition. It was a busy time for Johnson, who still had to play out the 2001 Busch season while preparing to take the next step.

He also had to maintain his relationship with the Herzogs despite the fact that he had already committed to Hendrick. The Herzogs had hoped to build a Winston Cup team of their own, but Johnson could not allow himself to feel as if he had betrayed them. He had too many other things to be concerned with. He had gone through too much in his career to feel guilty now.

"There have been a lot of times where I thought I was crazy, sacrificing even from back in high school," Johnson said. "But for some reason in the back of my head, I just was confident that things would work out. And they have. I've been able to chase my dreams and make all those sacrifices pay off. I was worried at the time: 'Boy, if racing doesn't work out, what am I going to have?"

"If you just work hard enough at it, and you're a good person, well, good things happen to good people. That's what I pride myself on, and it's all turned out. So, I'm really looking forward to this year and not having to worry about anything. I'm just going to drive racecars."[4]

Good things do indeed happen to good people. And great things were about to happen to Jimmie Johnson.

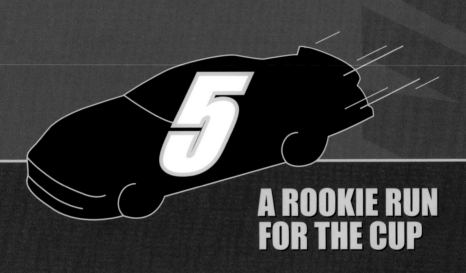

**T**alent and achievement do not necessarily go hand in hand.

The most gifted athletes do not always prove it through their performances. And some who do not boast the greatest natural ability accomplish the most.

NASCAR superstar Jeff Gordon and car owner Rick Hendrick saw tremendous talent in Jimmie Johnson when they signed him to a Winston Cup contract. It was that belief alone that prompted them to make such a bold move. Johnson had not exactly torn up the Busch series tracks.

In fact, he had yet to win a race while finishing tenth in overall points on that circuit in 2000. Though he managed to capture one event in 2001, Johnson only placed eighth in the final standings that year.

Such credentials did not necessarily warrant a promotion to the highest level of

## MOVING UP
**Johnson fared worse in qualifying but much better in the actual event in his second Daytona run of his rookie year. He qualified sixteenth for the July 6 race at that famed track but placed eighth.**

NASCAR racing. Others who finished higher would remain in the Busch series for the rest of their careers.

## PROVING HIMSELF

Twenty-six-year-old Johnson did not win anyone over when he made his Winston Cup debut in 2001. A wreck in the UAW-GM Quality 500 dropped him to thirty-ninth place. He followed that with a twenty-fifth at Homestead and twenty-ninth in Atlanta.

There was no reason to believe Johnson would do anything more than get his feet wet in his first full season in 2002. But he would justify his signing and prove the instincts of Gordon and Hendrick to be finely tuned. And he would do it when the wheels hit the asphalt for the first time that year.

Johnson stunned the racing world by driving to the pole position at the Daytona 500. For a rookie to be the fastest qualifier with a speed of 185.831 mph (299 kph), sheer talent had to play a primary role. He certainly could not credit experience.

**Johnson (left) and his brother Jarit (right) talk with their younger brother, Jesse, in his car. Jesse was preparing for a 2002 Bandolero series race.**

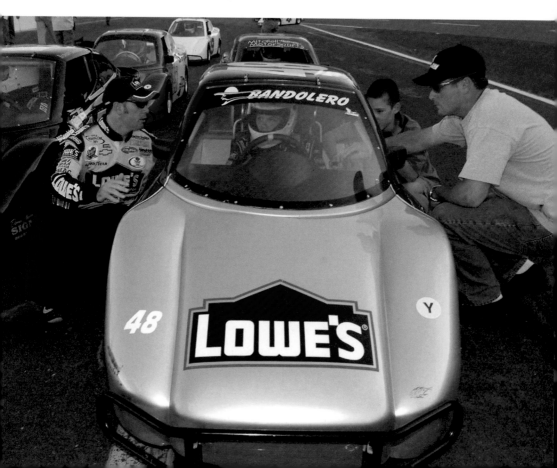

Following the Daytona qualifier, Johnson refused to praise the man in the mirror for his accomplishment. He had kind words for everyone involved.

"This is unbelievable," Johnson said. "You always think you have the ability to come out here and be competitive, but you just don't know until the right situation presents itself and you can showcase your talents. My hat's off to (crew chief) Chad (Knaus). We're both in a similar situation of trying to prove ourselves. I'm just blown away.

"The resources at Hendrick Motorsports—the chassis, the bodies, the support from (team sponsor) Lowe's—it all lets us do what we need to do on the racetrack and not worry about anything else."[1]

Johnson did not complete a fairy tale weekend by winning the Daytona 500, but he did finish a respectable fifteenth. After placing twenty-eighth in the Subway 400, he began a stretch of success few NASCAR rookies have ever enjoyed. He finished among the top seven in ten of the next twelve races, including his first Winston Cup race championship in the NAPA Auto Parts 500 and another in the MBNA Platinum 400 five weeks later.

Johnson had burst onto the scene with greater success than he had ever had in the Busch series, which is akin to a Major League Baseball player performing better than he did in the minors.

## TRADING ONE LOVE FOR ANOTHER
Johnson no longer rode motorcycles
competitively by the time he joined the
NASCAR circuit, but he admitted at that
time that he still loved racing them.

If his competition figured he would wilt in
the summer heat, they figured wrong. After winning
the MBNA Platinum 400, Johnson finished in the
top fifteen in thirteen of the next sixteen events. His
tenth-place performance in the Protection One 400
two weeks after his twenty-seventh birthday vaulted
him atop the overall point standings with less than
two months remaining in the season. He was the first
rookie ever to lead in the point standings.

"When Jimmie posted six top 10s in his first
12 races, we knew that Lowe's was happy with their
investment," Gordon said. "When he won his first
Winston Cup race in his 13th start, we looked like
geniuses. Three weeks later Jimmie won again. This
was unprecedented, and unbelievable. "I didn't win
my first race until well into my sophomore season
and I won the Rookie of the Year title. Jimmie had
two wins in his rookie year. Rick was happy, Lowe's
was thrilled, and I was breathing a little easier. This

car owner thing was a lot of pressure. Having Jimmie perform so well eliminated a lot of worry from my life."[2]

## GAINING POPULARITY

Along the way, Johnson impressed his fellow drivers and fans with his approach to the sport. His personality and intelligence also made him a media favorite. His parents had encouraged him to be a well-rounded person by downplaying the importance of winning and promoting hard work in all of his endeavors. What he had learned both on the track and away from it was starting to pay off.

"This season a young, articulate, well-mannered driver has combined the best of both worlds," wrote Larry Cothren of *Stock Car Racing Magazine*. "Jimmie Johnson is not only saying and doing the right things off the track, he's winning on the track at a pace ahead of even (Tony) Stewart's rookie campaign (in 1999).

"Johnson personifies the young, aggressive, winning driver that teams have searched for since Gordon lowered the bar in terms of when to expect success in the sport."[3]

Johnson did not win the Winston Cup crown that year. After winning the MBNA All-American Heroes 400 on September 22 for his third victory of the season, he placed no higher than sixth in his last eight events to fall to fifth in the overall point

## MIXING IT UP

In 2002, Jimmie Johnson, Jeff Gordon, and World Superbike champion Colin Edwards joined forces to win the Race of Champions Nations Cup, an annual event that pits the world's best rally, motorcycle, and circuit racers against one another.

standings. But for a driver who placed tenth and eighth, respectively, in his two years in the Busch series, such a performance as a rookie Winston Cup driver was nothing less than miraculous.

## A WINNING COMBINATION

The contribution of Knaus played a huge role in Johnson's success. The experience of the crew chief, particularly with Hendrick Motorsports, gave the rookie a knowledgeable and seasoned expert to work with before and during each event.

Knaus joined Hendrick Motorsports to work with Johnson, but he had previous experience with the organization. He originally worked as a fabricator, then as a tire changer and mechanic from 1993 to 1997 for highly successful crew chief Ray Evernham, who was a key component during Gordon's early glory years.

In 2002, many were comparing Johnson and Knaus with Gordon and Evernham. Knaus, however, was not ready to jump on that bandwagon at midseason.

"No, what Ray and Jeff did in Winston Cup racing, I don't think will ever be matched because they brought it . . . to a totally new level," Knaus said. "Those two guys brought Winston Cup racing to what it is today. I don't think we could ever revolutionize racing like they did.

"Ray was a very lucky man because if it wasn't for Jeff Gordon, Ray Evernham would not be who Ray Evernham is. I feel like I am just as lucky, because if it wasn't for Jimmie Johnson, I wouldn't be who I am today. Jimmie and I, the longer we work together, and the more time we spend together, the better friends we become."[4]

**Johnson (right) talks with crew chief Chad Knaus.**

By that time, Johnson had developed a comfortable routine. His immediate success allowed him to establish a pre-race ritual that he knew would work. Some of it was based on strategy, but most of it revolved around becoming emotionally and mentally geared for the event.

"Prior to each race, we have a meeting where we discuss strategy," Johnson said. "After that, I'll take a few minutes by myself in the team hauler to just clear my mind and focus my energy towards the race. This will include visualizing laps in my mind and hitting my marks. The races are so long, it doesn't do you a lot of good to get too excited over something.

"If you're starting towards the front, you get a little excited to try and get up there to lead the lap early and get those bonus points. But I try to stay relatively calm and just get excited and just get the good energy flowing. Get the energy flowing around my guys so they have a good, positive outlook on the race at hand. And have some fun."[5]

## TAKING THE RACING WORLD BY STORM

Johnson had enough fun to win *Stock Car Racing Magazine's* People's Choice Award for Biggest Surprise of 2002. Some believed his ability to rise to the level of competition had ended when he struggled to race with the best in the Busch series, but he dispelled that notion by nearly winning the Winston Cup as a rookie.

## A LIFE-ALTERING EXPERIENCE
After his first victory in 2002, Johnson received a call from fellow driver Kevin Harvick, who told him his life would never be the same. Johnson later admitted Harvick's prediction was correct.

Despite that success, some were cautioning Johnson and his fans to be realistic. Others had burst onto the scene but never reached any level of greatness.

"Some have already hailed him as the best rookie in memory," read an article in *Stock Car Racing Magazine*. "Then again, it wasn't too awful long ago that Tony Stewart and Kevin Harvick were standing the racing world on its ear as a rookie. Now it's Johnson who may set the standard for how rookies will be judged in time.

"Johnson's confidence grows with each new race, and that's enough to keep even the wily veterans on edge. Some may argue that this fellow will only be another flash in the pan in racing history, but

## A SPECIAL PLACE
Jimmie Johnson must love racing in the Northeast. Two of his three victories in 2003 were achieved in New Hampshire.

most likely we're witnessing the birth of the sport's next superstar."[6]

Such predictions are often premature and based on an athlete's early success. But in this case, it was right on the mark. Johnson was going to prove that the biggest surprise of the 2002 season and the next superstar of NASCAR were the same person.

# GROWING INTO HIS ROLE

**A**nything Jimmie Johnson achieved in 2002 was gravy. As a rookie, the perception was that what he did well was a pleasant surprise and what he did poorly could be written off by a lack of experience.

Johnson did exceed expectations by remaining in the hunt for a NASCAR championship until late in the season and finishing fifth overall. But the free pass was no longer offered in 2003. As a second-year Winston Cup driver, Johnson discovered that anything less than significant improvement would be considered a disappointment.

## SOPHOMORE SLUMP?

Though Johnson raced well at times during the first half of the year, he was plagued by poor performances. He placed out of the top ten in fourteen of the first twenty-three events in 2003. His twenty-seventh-place finish in the GFS Marketplace 400 on August 17 dropped him to sixth place in the overall standings.

That is when Johnson began running full speed. Though he captured only the Sylvania 300 title during the final two months of the year, he finished in the top seven in eleven of the final thirteen events. In fact, he took second or third in the last six races. By the time the smoke had cleared, he was second overall behind runaway winner Matt Kenseth.

He had achieved significant improvement as a sophomore. Though Johnson received a taste of the competition as a rookie, he learned a great deal about it when he battled Dale Earnhardt, Jr., Ryan Newman, and Gordon for second place down the stretch. It had taken all season to find the consistency required to remain in the upper realm of Winston Cup driving. But he had discovered the secret far earlier than nearly all the other younger drivers.

"Maybe in the last few years, the speed has been with these younger drivers, but maybe not the consistency," Johnson said. "Everybody out there is a very smart racecar driver in learning the dos and don'ts and how to be consistent and not get into wrecks and have problems. I think the young faces you see will continue to be there.

"But at the same time it's not about age. Look at (46-year-old) Bill Elliott. He's been strong for the last three months (in 2003). It's about communication and it's about people."[1]

And that is where Johnson felt his greatest appreciation. He understood that without a superior crew and strong backing, he was just another driver.

"It was just a great year for the entire Lowe's team," he said following the 2003 season. "I never in my wildest dreams expected to have six victories (for his career). The Winston, all the poles, and a fifth-place finish last year, and a second-place finish this year. But we're here. I'm just getting all I can every day, every lap, and so are (crew chief Chad Knaus) and the entire team.

"We have a great relationship, great equipment, and great sponsors. You hear everybody say that stuff, but it really is the truth. The sport is about people. The top teams all have the same equipment. It's all about people. I'm so fortunate to have the crew that I do. They've made a sophomore finish second this year."[2]

## LEARNING FROM EXPERIENCE

Johnson's relationship with Gordon was particularly helpful. Though only four years younger than the

Johnson's crew works on his car during a pit stop at Lowe's Motor Speedway on May 30, 2004.

four-time Winston Cup champion, Johnson was nine years behind in experience. Gordon, who entered the racing scene with a reputation for recklessness on the track, taught Johnson the importance of staying focused and combining aggressiveness with caution.

Gordon also preached patience. Since Winston Cup races are longer than those in the Busch series, an eventual shift in momentum is more likely. And there is more time to work out mechanical problems.

"(Gordon) said you have many opportunities to work on your car," Johnson said. "If you can stay on the lead lap, stay patient, and keep working on your car, crazy things can happen. The race turns around, comes your way, and you can salvage good finishes out of bad days."[3]

## WINNING IN HIS PERSONAL LIFE, TOO

There were many more good days to come for Johnson, including in his personal life. Gordon played a key role in that as well. In 2003, Gordon played matchmaker between his young friend and model Chandra Janway, who became Johnson's wife a little more than a year later.

Johnson did not need any prodding when it came to courting his new girlfriend. Before he met Chandra, he was living the life of a bachelor and enjoying the freedom. But once he laid eyes on Chandra, he began to think differently.

**Chandra and Jimmie celebrate his win at the Brickyard on August 6, 2006.**

"Once I saw her, that was pretty much the end for me," Johnson said. "Then, as I got to know her, that's when it really grabbed me. The last thing on my mind was settling down, but when I met her, it just stopped me in my tracks."[4]

Johnson's personal and professional life was expanding in other directions as well. Both articulate in front of a microphone and experienced and comfortable in front of a camera, he was sought after by the media.

He had become respected enough both on and off the track to be invited to be a presenter at the nationally televised 2003 Country Music Television

**TIME FOR CHORES**
Jimmie Johnson considers Monday as his only day off during the week, but he finds time to do laundry and other personal chores on Wednesdays.

awards in Nashville, Tennessee. He handled his duty flawlessly.

### USING HIS TALENTS WISELY

It is impossible to handle racing flawlessly. All Johnson could do on the track was minimize mistakes and maximize potential. But he was not raised with a "win-at-all-costs" mentality. He understood that all he could do was give each race, each moment, his best shot. And if he could look in the mirror that night with a clear conscience, he could sleep soundly.

The work ethic and sense of priorities instilled into Johnson by his parents remain with him today. After the 2003 season, he spoke about what his first two seasons on the Winston Cup circuit meant to him. Second place in his second year, after all, is hardly something to be ashamed of. Considering he was no more than an also-ran throughout his two years in the Busch series, he had opened many eyes on the NASCAR circuit.

"Being the first loser doesn't bother me too much," Johnson said. "I didn't expect to be in this position. Of course I wanted to win the championship (in 2003). I wanted to win it (in 2002) and do something no one's ever done. It doesn't mean we're not putting in everything that we can. But we're in a position where we don't need to put any additional pressure on ourselves.

"If you look at history, it usually takes three, four, or five years to get the driver and the team into championship form. Maybe next year will be that special year for us. It takes a lot of luck. If you look at Matt Kenseth's year, he's been fast and done all the right things, but he's had flat tires at the right point in time and only been caught up in one

## A DIFFERENT ADVENTURE
**Jeff Gordon accompanied Jimmie Johnson on Johnson's first scuba diving expedition before the 2004 season.**

or two wrecks and one blown engine. That's hard to do. We'll give it 100 percent (in 2004) and see what happens."[5]

The daily routine of Winston Cup racing was making Johnson more comfortable. He had become familiar with the tracks and was more in tune with Knaus and the rest of the team. He had overcome one major obstacle that all sports figures fear—the sophomore slump.

He also began to understand that talent does not always translate into the ultimate success. The Winston Cup circuit featured so many tremendous drivers that he would have to maximize his own abilities and even be presented with a little bit of luck to ever win a championship. The popularity of NASCAR was infusing the sport with a greater number of talented drivers than ever before.

Some of the NASCAR veterans had given Johnson plenty of opportunities to test his skills against them.

"It's weird to be racing alongside of guys and beating guys that were my idols growing up. Last season in Darlington, I was coming off pit road with the No. 88 behind me, and we all know how good Dale Jarrett is at Darlington. Three laps into that run, I looked in my rearview mirror and I was pulling away from him. I was amazed, and I think that was one instance when I started building some confidence in the fact that I could run with guys like Jeff Gordon, Mark Martin and Dale Jarrett on a regular basis."[6]

As the 2003 season wound down, Johnson began considering what it would take to earn a crown.

"I do have a better understanding of the difficulties in competing and winning races and winning championships," he said. "With our being a rookie team last year, the worst thing we could do was have that pressure on our shoulders. We were putting ourselves in that position by not thinking or worrying about that. As soon as that pressure starts to creep in, then you change.

"That's what we're going to try to avoid this year. With the future at hand, who knows when this opportunity will happen again? I think (veteran Winston Cup driver) Mark Martin has finally realized that, and we all know how hard he's been on himself for years for not getting a championship. You can't deny the man the effort and dedication he's put into it, but it just hasn't happened for him yet. I don't want to find myself or my team in that situation."[7]

It is easier said than done, however, as Johnson was soon to discover.

Jimmie Johnson understood only one career objective remained when the 2004 season began.

That was to win a title in what was now known as the Nextel Cup.

He had already been established as a premier driver. He had already finished second in the overall standings. He had even played a role in making NASCAR the fastest-growing sport in America.

If individual brilliance in the vast majority of events determined champions, Johnson would have sped away with the crown that year. He finished in the top six in twenty-one of thirty-six races and won eight. He placed sixth or higher in five straight events during three separate stretches.

But titles are earned by compiling the most points. A brutal two-month period from August to October sent Johnson plummeting from first to ninth place overall.

## A STUNNING TURN OF EVENTS

Johnson appeared doomed, but he rallied in the fall to charge toward the top. He earned consecutive victories in the UAW-GM Quality 500, Subway 500, and Bass Pro Shops MBNA 500 in late October, won the Mountain Dew Southern 500 two weeks later, and finished the season by placing second in the Ford 400. That allowed him to finish the season second in the points standings behind Kurt Busch.

## OOPS!

*Stock Car Racing Magazine* writer Larry Cothren predicted Jimmie Johnson would win the Nextel Cup in 2004. He picked actual winner Kurt Busch to finish twelfth in the overall standings.

**Johnson crosses the finish line to win the Subway 500 on October 24, 2004, at Martinsville Speedway.**

Each journey for a NASCAR driver is different. What Johnson learned by placing second in 2004 was not the same as what he learned by taking the same spot in 2003. He understood now the importance of consistency.

The horrible stretch late in the year took the ultimate success out of Johnson's hands. He needed others to falter to get back into the Chase for the Nextel Cup title. He was fortunate to have finished just eight points behind Busch.

"I didn't feel (the championship hopes) were over, but I'm a realist and I knew it was out of our control," Johnson said in mid-November of that year.

"We were going to need mistakes made by everybody ahead of us to catch up. And everybody did make those mistakes.

"And I have to admit, I'm pretty shocked by that. I know some mistakes were made, and other things were just racing incidents. I didn't expect (Hendrick Motorsports teammate) Jeff Gordon to have any trouble, and they broke a gear, so it's nothing anybody can control, but I'm shocked those guys have had bad races. I thought somebody would make it clean."[1]

That is not the only thing that shocked Johnson. He was also stunned by a plane crash in Southwest Virginia on October 24 that killed ten Hendrick Motorsports employees and family members. Among those who perished were John Hendrick, company president and brother of Rick Hendrick, and NASCAR team owner and John's son Ricky Hendrick.

The group had been traveling to the Subway 500 that weekend in Martinsville, but heavy clouds obscured visibility and the plane struck a mountain.

Johnson won the race that Sunday and followed it up the next weekend with his third consecutive victory. But his heart was too heavy to enjoy his climb back toward the top of the Nextel Cup standings. He had vaulted from eighth place to second in three weeks, an improbable feat that late in the year, but Johnson found it impossible to make racing a priority.

"Winning Martinsville . . . it doesn't even seem like we won Martinsville," Johnson said. "I don't even remember the Martinsville race because of everything that took place. And then Atlanta, it was fitting. It put a smile on Rick's face and the families involved and throughout Hendrick Motorsports.

"So I look at those races and can't really clump them together and think of what we accomplished. I know that we won three in a row and that sounds good and feels good, but with what took place it just doesn't have the same feel that you'd expect."[2]

**Johnson's car honored the memory of his teammates who died in a 2004 plane crash.**

**A mourner reflects prior to a candlelight vigil and service held for victims of the Hendrick Motorsports plane crash.**

It was in the emotional shadow of the plane crash that Johnson married the love of his life. He exchanged wedding vows with Chandra on the island of St. Bart's in the Caribbean on December 11.

His life was changing quickly. The loss of his colleagues and friends from Hendrick Motorsports altered his perspective and showed him how fragile life could be. He welcomed the permanent and steady love he received from marriage. Plus Chandra had stirred up emotions in him he had never previously felt. He had wanted to fall in love and get married, but it took a special woman to help him come to grips with that feeling.

"It's something I've always wanted, but I couldn't see it until I met (Chandra)," Johnson said.

"Then after meeting (her) I couldn't see anything else. It really was cool for me to experience and how it showed—how that desire to be with one person shows up, and to be married and everything that goes with it—how that just grabs you. It grabbed me, and I'm loving every minute of it."[3]

## THE KEYS TO SUCCESS

The whirlwind of events at the end of 2004 took a while for Johnson to put into perspective. He had undergone the worst driving slump of his career, dealt with the death of his Hendrick Motorsports friends and family, attempted to enjoy one of the greatest stretch runs in NASCAR history, and gotten married, all during a five-month period.

During that off-season, however, he had time to reflect on what he had achieved in the final months of the 2004 season and refocus on what was becoming an elusive goal—winning a Nextel Cup championship.

Johnson knew that if he could only bottle all the ingredients used during the dominant stretches of 2004 and at least minimize the mistakes made from early August to

**DID YOU KNOW?**

Jeff Gordon, who helped develop the relationship between Jimmie Johnson and Chandra Janway, was in the wedding party when the two got married in December 2004.

early October, he would be considered a favorite to take the title.

The growing popularity of NASCAR throughout the country had translated into the infusion of greater talent than ever and incredible balance. But Johnson had the formula for success. He simply needed to channel it every day. And so did his teammates.

"I'm prouder looking at what we did at the end of the year, with the competition how it was and the parity in our sport, because we didn't have the fastest car in every one of those races we won," Johnson said. "In a few of them, definitely we were the car to beat.

"(Crew chief Chad Knaus) made the right adjustments, he put me out there with good track position, and I drove my butt off. So it showed me at the end of the year that you can't give up until the last lap. Even though there's parity in our sport, there's still so much human involvement where mistakes can be made on anyone's part to change the outcome of a race. That's why our sport's so popular."[4]

The competitive nature developed between individual drivers is another reason for its popularity. Johnson had been

**ROCKY ROAD**
In 2004, Jimmie Johnson placed thirty-sixth or lower in five races.

The car of Elliott Sadler (38, top left) is spun sideways on the 19th lap by Jimmie Johnson (48, top center) during the 2005 UAW-Ford 500 at Talladega Superspeedway.

raised to embrace a strong work ethic over a win-at-all-cost attitude, which kept him away from bitter rivalries. But finishing second twice had heightened his desire to win. Early in 2005, his fellow drivers began hinting that Johnson had crossed the line from aggressive to reckless.

## ANGRY ACCUSATIONS

Johnson began the year on a roll, placing in the top eight in the first seven races, including a first-place finish in Las Vegas. NASCAR deducted twenty-five points because his roof was deemed too low, but after the first two months of the 2005 season, he was solidly entrenched atop the overall points standings. He would remain there through July.

But on April 3, he collided with Jeff Burton at Bristol Motor Speedway. Burton's car eventually slid up the track, where he had a head-on collision with Kurt Busch. Burton spoke angrily about the incident after the race.

"He's got to be better than that," Burton said. "He can't be doing that, and I won't put up with it."[5]

Two weeks later in Phoenix, Johnson's car appeared to tap Tony Stewart's car from behind. Stewart's car spun and took out three other drivers. Johnson and Stewart took turns trading accusations after that event.

"The only way you spin like that is when a guy jacks you up like that going into (Turn) 3," Stewart said. "I don't know what he was doing. He was running guys up and down the racetrack. He about ran (Dale Earnhardt, Jr.) into the wall."[6]

Johnson answered in no uncertain terms. "The last three or four weeks I've raced with (Tony), when I get to him he's mad that I'm

## TROUBLE ON THE TRACK

Johnson was knocked out of seven races in 2004 due to accidents or engine failures, the highest total of his six-year career.

going by and he starts (gesturing) and running me all over the place," Johnson said. "I don't know why he gets so (mad) whenever I'm around him. I end up being the whipping boy every time I get to him, it seems like."

Earnhardt then blamed Johnson for a multi-car wreck at Talladega in May.

"If there was an idiot out there, it was Johnson," he said.

Johnson, who responded jokingly that Chandra called him an idiot every day, suspected that his competitors were trying to rattle him since he was still leading the points standings.

"No matter if you're the points leader or not, your target gets bigger and bigger," said fellow driver Jeremy Mayfield. "You've got more people shooting at your target than what you realize. To win the championship, you need to race like you've been racing, not change your ways after you become the points leader."[7]

Johnson admitted to being surprised by the controversies. He had never faced such criticism during his racing career. But he was comfortable enough with the man he saw in the mirror every night to place the blame entirely on himself.

"It makes me uncomfortable to hear things and to be accused of whatever it is," Johnson said. "I know that there's a lot of fans out there who don't like

me. They're wearing red (Dale Earnhardt, Jr.'s color).
I know there are a lot of fans out there wearing blue
(Johnson's color) that do like me.

"It makes me think harder about who I am,
what I am, and the type of driver I am. I'm not going
to let anybody's opinion change what I do or who I
am."[8]

Johnson could not let off-the-track sniping
affect him. He had to focus on driving. He had a
championship that needed to be won.

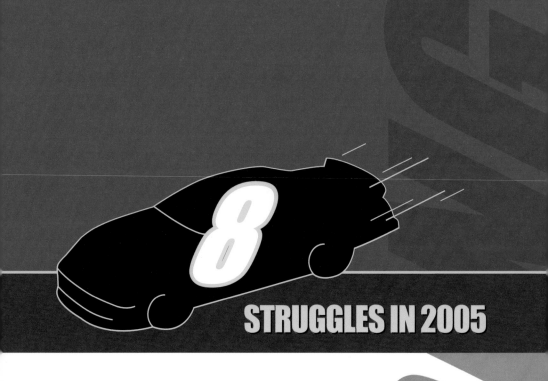

**O**n May 29, 2005, Jimmie Johnson sat in front of the cameras and microphones and fielded questions from the media.

He had just nipped Bobby Labonte to win his third consecutive Coca-Cola 600. He was solidly entrenched in first place in the Nextel Cup point standings. He had finished in the top eight in nine of twelve races that season.

The Coca-Cola 600 was the kind of race that had catapulted NASCAR into the American spotlight. Several accidents resulted in a total of twenty-two caution flags. And down the stretch, Johnson and Labonte streaked side by side toward the finish line. Johnson zoomed across it a split-second earlier than his rival.

Johnson's thoughts took a leap back two months to the Golden Corral 500 in Atlanta, in which he finished second after a furious finish. These races were what NASCAR was all about. Johnson's competitive spirit had been brought out.

"In all my years of racing, I've never seen anything like this," he told the assembled media. "I thought we were in such good shape if we could just stay out of trouble, and then the caution got us. So many cautions.

## A STAND-UP GUY

NASCAR official Jim Hunter publicly defended Johnson after he had been criticized by fellow drivers following two April 2005 accidents.

"Usually here you see a long green run, but everybody's trying to plan a strategy based on that. It was just a crazy race. There were just a few laps to go, and we could have finished 10th or 11th. I thought we were happy. So, it was a strange race. A great race as it turned out."[1]

## AN UP-AND-DOWN SEASON

Johnson had to temper his enthusiasm and optimism. He had been there before. He had spent months at a time dominating the Winston Cup field, only to see it all slip away in a haze of poor performances and engine failures. He did not want that to happen again in 2005.

But, alas, it did.

Once again, Johnson wilted in the heat of the summer. He placed sixth or better in four of the six races following the Coca-Cola 600, then took a respectable thirteenth and twelfth, respectively, in the next two events.

When the cars lined up for the Allstate 400 at the Brickyard in Indianapolis on August 7, Johnson was hanging on to first place in the overall points standings. When he was knocked out of that race with sixteen laps remaining, he dropped into second. He would not stop falling until late September.

Johnson bottomed out at the Sylvania 300 on September 18. Though he placed a strong eighth in that New Hampshire event, he had fallen into sixth place overall. After sitting atop the standings most of the year, he was threatened

**DID YOU KNOW?**

Jimmie Johnson maintained a top-five spot overall through the entire 2005 season, except after the September 28 race in New Hampshire, when he slipped to sixth.

with his worst overall standing since his rookie season.

He understood by that time what it took to win consistently. He understood how quickly fortunes could turn in Nextel Cup racing. He just could not seem to avoid the slumps that all but killed his chances at a championship year after year.

As in previous seasons, Johnson made another furious fall rush to the top. An accident in the season-ending Ford 400 caused a fortieth-place finish and doomed Johnson to fifth place overall for the year. That spot might cause others to turn cartwheels, but it was nothing exceptional for Johnson. Every near miss at a championship heightened his desire to win one. Some might have doubted if he ever would, but neither he nor crew chief Chad Knaus were among them.

"You know, I'm proud of the team," Johnson said after the season. "We've been in championship contention for three years so far in our career at the Cup level. To win the championship is what we're here for and coming so close, there's really nowhere to go in our mind than up to win the championship."[2]

**NEW RULES**

The Chase for the Cup, initiated by NASCAR in 2004, erased the point totals for the top ten drivers and allowed them to start over for the final ten events.

**Johnson talks with crew chief Chad Knaus during qualifying runs at Daytona International Speedway.**

Knaus expressed optimism as well, but it was tempered by the disappointment of another lost opportunity.

"It's sad. It's disappointing," said the crew chief. "You work a long time all season long to get this championship, and we've been in this position since this team was first born. Since 2002, we've battled for the championship. So, as long as we keep doing that, consistency will sooner or later pay off for us. And we'll get that trophy. It just hasn't been meant to be just yet.

"We can bounce back from anything, easy. We've gone through more trials and tribulations as a team than any other team has possibly tried to overcome, and we have overcome it all."[3]

## FINDING HIS OWN VOICE

Meanwhile, Johnson wanted racing fans to know what makes him tick. Johnson did not mind being linked as a teammate with Gordon, who is either adored or hated by many racing fans. He also understood that the controversies he had endured both on and off the track in 2005 come with the territory.

**DID YOU KNOW?**

Johnson admitted he was just as nervous to be a presenter at the 2003 Country Music Television Awards as he was when he drove in the Daytona 500 that year.

But he also believed that followers of NASCAR did not know him well as a person. So he used his verbal talents, outgoing personality, and media experience to launch a weekly show on XM Satellite's NASCAR Radio, which debuted in February 2006. Johnson not only discussed the weekly happenings of the sport both on and off the track, he also spoke about his interests, such as music and other personal likes and dislikes.

It was not a financial decision. Johnson was making millions of dollars a year as one of the premier drivers on the Nextel Cup circuit. Both he and the sport had reached such a level of popularity that fans wanted to know all about their favorite drivers.

"For a few years I've been searching for the right outlet to give people an opportunity to get to know a side of me away from the racetrack," Johnson said when announcing the radio program. "XM approached me with the idea of having a national weekly radio show, and it was a perfect fit."[4]

But fans were still most interested in racing issues related to Johnson. He had earned a reputation as the most successful driver to have never won a championship. Though he had yet to win a Daytona 500 or Brickyard race, he had never struggled

**DID YOU KNOW?**

Jimmie Johnson's sponsor, Lowe's, announced a partnership with the United Services Organization (USO) soon after the Iraq war began late in 2003. The USO supports troops by providing morale, entertainment and recreation-type services to members of the U.S. military worldwide. The USO is the way the American public supports the troops.

to win individual events. He had celebrated in Victory Lane as a rookie.

But his desire to win a title heightened every year. He remained proud of his and his team's accomplishments. But there was that feeling of emptiness, of a barren spot in the trophy case.

"I've won a lot of big, big events, and they're very special," he had said before the 2005 season. "But there's nothing like a championship. There's nothing like having that respect through the garage, in the media, with the fans, of being THE guy."[5]

**Drivers who made the Chase for the Nextel Cup pose on September 10, 2005. Among them is Jimmie Johnson, back row, second from left.**

Even before he could slip into his racecar for the kickoff of the 2006 season, controversy struck again. Knaus was suspended by NASCAR authorities for a rules violation found in a post-qualifying inspection for the Daytona 500. It was discovered that the rear windshield had been altered, which allowed more air to deflect off the rear spoiler and increase the speed of the car.

Johnson, however, was still allowed to race in the Daytona 500. And when that event had been run, he had earned his greatest single-race victory in the most prestigious event on the NASCAR circuit.

In other years, winning Daytona might not have proven to be a preview of a championship season. But there was something different brewing in 2006.

# AN UP-AND-DOWN SEASON

**J**immie Johnson is no stranger to a love-hate relationship with NASCAR fans. As a young Californian he is considered by many an outsider bucking tradition.

His critics believe that the sport was built by rural and small-town southerners, good old boys who rose through the ranks through hard work and determination.

A Californian who rose through the ranks through hard work and determination? It just was not the same.

Like fellow Californian Jeff Gordon, Johnson did not fit the mold. But he had become accustomed to such petty dislikes.

What he was not used to was fending off allegations of cheating. The suspension of Knaus for inspection violations during the Daytona 500 qualifying event in 2006 weighed heavily upon Johnson and his teammates. Though he was cleared to compete in the most anticipated race of the season, how well could he concentrate?

Quite well, as it turned out. Johnson captured the Daytona 500. Johnson did not feel the victory was dampened by the suspension of his crew chief. In fact, he expressed quite the opposite. It felt sweeter because there was more to overcome.

"Right now I have so much pride in my race team, what we have accomplished today with the circumstances we've been through," Johnson said in the post-race interview with the media. "This is a well-prepared team, a team that was very hungry and wanted to make a statement today. We stepped up and got the job done, and I'm very proud of the guys."[1]

## TEAMWORK

Only two championship driver-crew chief teams have stayed together longer than Johnson and Knaus —Tony Stewart and Greg Zipadelli, as well as Matt Kenseth and Robbie Reiser.

## DEALING WITH CONSEQUENCES

Johnson was not making any excuses for Knaus. He accepted the penalty handed down by the NASCAR authorities. He understood that he would probably have to perform without Knaus for another three weeks. He did not complain that it was unfair. He did believe, however, that what he and his team accomplished without their crew chief was tremendous.

"If you think about what we overcame, and the pressure that's on any team, in any sport, if they were faced with something like this, this a huge, huge statement, something that I'm very proud of," Johnson said in the press conference following his Daytona 500 triumph. "We play within a set of rules. Chad broke the rules. He's admitted that. He's in Charlotte watching the race today. He missed the event. We're serving our penalty. We're doing everything we can do. We stepped up today and won the biggest race in our sport, and it is something I am so proud of."[2]

When he continued to be peppered with questions regarding that issue, Johnson finally showed a bit of anger. He believed such questions were justified after the qualifying inspection, but not after a clean victory that day.

So when he was told fellow driver Ryan Newman had been critical of him, Johnson answered in a manner that was not typical of him.

Johnson celebrates as he climbs out of his car in Victory Lane after winning the 2006 Daytona 500.

**Johnson and Jeff Gordon talk with Johnson's temporary crew chief, Darian Grubb (center).**

"I kind of view it as jealousy, and he doesn't have a crew chief in there working hard enough to make his cars as good," Johnson said. "If you look at what place he took last year, we had an appeal overturned, which has never been done in the sport. We were complimented for the shocks that we built and designed at Dover. So it just depends on how you look at it.

"This team has worked way too hard to even have those kind of comments thrown at them, and I'm going to be very defensive over it. This team works way too hard; all the teams do in the garage area. I'm disappointed that Ryan has to come in here and make some different statements and try to tarnish what we accomplished today. I'm very proud of this team, and we've worked very hard for what we've got."[3]

Johnson grabbed the momentum he had gained at Daytona and raced ahead with it. He followed up with a second-place finish in the Auto Club 500 and a victory in the UAW-DaimlerChrysler 400, both utilizing backup crew chief Darian Grubb, who emerged as a hero throughout the ordeal.

"The great thing about the decision we made with Darian to come in and crew this was his involvement with the team for so many years," Johnson said after the Daytona victory. "He's worked alongside Chad as our race engineer and was involved in all the conversations when Chad and I would talk about the handling of the car (and) the different things I communicate to Chad.

"To put Darian in was, in my eyes, the best thing to do for this team because the communication has already been started. We've been working together for three, almost four years. We know each other. Darian has a lot of respect inside the team. So it really was the best decision."[4]

## A DREAM COME TRUE

By the time Knaus returned from his suspension, the team was in first place overall, but that had become standard for Johnson. He had spent two months atop the standings in 2004 and four months there in 2005. Now, they would no longer be satisfied unless they won the championship.

**Johnson kisses the bricks after winning the Allstate 400 at Indianapolis Motor Speedway.**

The positive energy continued for quite a while in 2006. Johnson captured the Aaron's 499 at Talladega on May 1 to slide back into first place overall, a position he maintained through August. He placed in the top ten in ten of eleven events from mid-May to early August.

Johnson peaked on August 6 with a victory in the Allstate 400 at the Brickyard at the famed

**TRAVELING COMPANIONS**
Jimmie Johnson and his wife, Chandra, took a three-week vacation to South Africa following the 2005 season.

Indianapolis Motor Speedway. That triumph was sweetened by memories of his past failures at that track. After a respectable ninth-place finish there in 2002, he had placed no higher than eighteenth. And in both 2004 and 2005, an engine failure and accident had prevented him from even completing the race.

The Indianapolis Motor Speedway is a legendary site in auto racing. Winning there not only solidified Johnson's hold on first place in the Nextel Cup standings, it also gave him chills. He crossed the finish line ahead of the competition despite a blown tire on Lap 40.

"I never thought I would ever win at this racetrack," he admitted in the post-race interview. "We had such a drought at this track and now I have the victory.

**DID YOU KNOW?**
Team owner Rick Hendrick brought Johnson and Knaus together for a meeting before the 2006 season to ensure that they were on the same page after the disappointing finish in 2005.

Johnson does a victory spin after winning the Nextel All-Star Challenge race in May 2006.

I was really worried when we had the tire problem, but I cannot believe how good this Monte Carlo was today. I didn't even think of the championship today. I wanted to win this race, and I'm going to pucker up and kiss those bricks."[5]

The triumph proved an emotional one for Johnson, who in his youth in California was a huge fan of Indy Car champion Rick Mears. He dreamed of following in his Mears' tire tracks. He just never dreamed it would happen in a NASCAR event.

"When I was a kid, I thought I would come here in an Indy Car like my hero, Rick Mears," Johnson said. "I can't believe I won it in a stock car.

"This track has been an emotional disaster for us; some type of disaster from blowing an engine to hitting the wall. We've left here and it's taken the wind out of our sails. I just can't believe we overcame all the things we have at this racetrack and the challenges we had today and won."[6]

## LOW TIMES

If Johnson thought the victory at the Brickyard would prevent a fall collapse, however, he thought wrong. He finished no higher than tenth in the next nine races. He completed all but one of those events but fared poorly in all of them. He remained in first place after poor performances in the AMD at The Glen, GFS Marketplace 400, and Sharpie 500 but dropped into

## WINS DO NOT ENSURE TITLES

Johnson earned more victories and top-ten finishes than Tony Stewart, Matt Kenseth, and Kurt Busch from 2002 to 2005. Yet all three won Nextel Cup titles while Johnson had finished no higher than second.

second overall after an eleventh-place finish in the Sony HD 500.

The free-fall was just beginning. He finished a woeful thirty-ninth in the Sylvania 300 in New Hampshire on September 17 and plummeted from second to ninth in the points standings. Johnson stood in eighth place overall after an accident knocked him out at the UAW-Ford 500 in Talladega on October 8.

What made that crash particularly frustrating was that Johnson was in position to win the race. As he tried to pass Earnhardt, Jr. for the lead on the final lap, his car was bumped by Hendrick Motorsports teammate Brian Vickers. Both Johnson and Earnhardt, Jr. spun out, allowing Vickers to race past both for the victory.

"It's racing," Johnson said following that event. "It's like I've said all along. I know it was not intentional. We had a great opportunity to make up some points. But life goes on. We've got to worry about this weekend.

"I really just have to go out and do all that I can and score as many points as possible and see how it falls into place. We're pretty far out, and it's going to be tough to make up the deficit that we have. But the way this Chase has started and the way every year the Chase has been that I've been a part of it, it's so unpredictable. Anything can happen."[7]

Indeed, anything could happen. Little did anyone know how prophetic that statement would prove to be.

# CROWNED A CHAMPION

**N**othing short of a miraculous finish to the 2006 season would result in a championship for Jimmie Johnson. It would take strong runs in all six races down the stretch. And it would take quite a bit of luck. After all, he had seven drivers to pass in less than a month and a half.

His march to glory was both inspiring and methodical. He placed second in the Bank of America 500, but that merely served to move him up one spot to seventh overall.

Johnson followed that by winning the Subway 500. Suddenly

## DIGGING A HOLE
**Johnson fell 165 points behind in the third week of the Chase for the Cup in 2006 before starting his comeback.**

he was third in the points standings. What seemed impossible two weeks earlier appeared quite possible after that triumph.

Following that race, he was asked about his chances of winning the title. Such questions had become old hat to Johnson. He had been in position to win the crown nearly every year. He did not know how to answer without repeating himself.

Johnson was not one to believe any season was a disaster if a championship had not been earned. But he did not want to sound as if he would be thrilled at another second-place finish.

"We'll just keep racing," he said after the Subway 500. "This team has done a great job. We've got a lot of speed and haven't had the finishes to show for it. Regardless of how this year finishes out, I'm very proud of this race team. Lowe's and all the team have worked really hard to get us what we need. Hendrick Motorsports has given Chad everything we need at the racetrack."[1]

## FINDING INSPIRATION

The Subway 500 win in Martinsville had added meaning for Johnson. It marked the two-year anniversary of the crash that took the life of ten Hendrick Motorsports colleagues. That bitter memory gave Johnson added inspiration in his quest for a Nextel Cup championship.

And he performed like it in every event with the 2006 title on the line. Johnson vaulted into second place overall by placing second the following week in the Bass Pro Shops 500. He sneaked into the lead in the points standings by finishing second yet again, this time in the Dickies 500.

The pressure was clearly on. But Johnson either did not feel it or he did not want to admit it existed. After his Subway 500 win and a month in which he finished no lower than second in any race, he spoke about the comeback from his brutal early-fall stretch. He believed that if he had not enjoyed and embraced the challenge, he would have been doomed.

"We've had so much fun racing for this since we got down," Johnson said. "We just want to keep having fun."[2]

That Johnson could take such a mental and emotional approach with so much at stake spoke volumes about his upbringing, about the days when his father leaned against a tree, seemingly without a care in the world, while his son zoomed around various

California tracks. Johnson once again understood that he needed only to answer to the man he saw in the mirror. He could enjoy himself despite the pressure if he felt comfortable that he was putting forth maximum effort.

In 2006, that attitude would translate into the greatest achievement of his career. He solidified his hold on first place in the points standings with his third consecutive second-place finish, this time in the Checker Auto Parts 500. He entered the season-ending Ford 400 with a 63-point lead on Matt Kenseth. Johnson just needed a decent run to earn his first crown.

## PATIENCE PAYS OFF

Johnson's ninth-place finish in that race clinched the title, but it did not come without its dramatic setbacks. His crew dropped a lugnut on his front tire during a pit stop on Lap 118. Johnson stopped himself from bolting back on the track. The stop cost him time and ten spots, but it could have been disastrous had he been overanxious and decided not to wait.

Earlier in his career, he might have made that mistake. But he was a cool veteran now. Even in making such a split-second decision, he knew that he could not afford to get knocked out of the race.

**Johnson raises the Nextel Cup championship trophy in 2006.**

In the end, it was Johnson and Knaus celebrating the Nextel Cup championship. They had jealously watched others dance for joy in years past after that same event. But on November 19, 2006, they were the ones popping champagne.

"This team has really come into its own the last year," Knaus said. "We've had to battle back from a lot of weird stuff. There's never been a team to come into this division with as much pressure on it as this team. When we came here in 2002, we had Jeff Gordon's championship-winning racecars (from his 2001 title run), so Jimmie and I and the team had to step up. And to win the championship in 2006 is just incredible."[3]

## GIVING BACK

Johnson celebrated heartily. He received more media attention than ever, but he refused to allow his success to change him. He began paying more attention to the Jimmie Johnson Charitable

**DID YOU KNOW?**

**Johnson and Knaus have signed contracts that will keep them with Hendrick Motorsports through the 2010 season.**

**A SPECIAL DAY**

**The California Speedway honored Johnson for his Nextel Cup title with a celebration in San Diego on January 31, 2007. San Diego mayor Jerry Sanders declared that day "Jimmie Johnson Day" in his city.**

**Members of Johnson's crew pose for photographs following the last race of the 2006 season.**

Foundation, which he had initiated in February 2006 to help families across the country. He and Chandra founded the organization with the motivation of improving the lives of children in need.

"Chandra and I have been very blessed," Johnson said. "We get to do what we enjoy in life, and that is something we don't take for granted. We have incredibly supportive friends and family, and we feel that I have the best fans in our sport. It is in that spirit of thankfulness that we launched the Jimmie Johnson Foundation in February 2006.

"As we begin to think about how we could give back, we found there are so many worthy

Johnson waves the checkered flag after winning the Allstate 400 on August 6, 2006.

causes. All of them are deserving of our time and effort, so concentrating on a few was a very tough decision. One thing that Chandra and I knew for sure was that we wanted to help families, particularly children. Our mission is to help those in need achieve their dreams."[4]

Several organizations benefited from the generosity of Johnson and his wife. Included was the Victory Junction Gang Camp, which provides camping experiences to children with life-threatening illnesses. More well-known charities such as the Make-A-Wish Foundation, for which they serve on the National Advisory Council, and the American Red Cross, are also targeted by the couple.

## BACK TO BACK

When Johnson returned to Daytona to start the 2007 season, memories of his victory at the 2006 Daytona 500 flooded back. But he quickly changed his focus to to trying to repeat as Nextel Cup champion.

"It's been a great emotional ride for myself and the team," Johnson said. "Last night I took the guys to dinner and we just sat around and had some fun and talked about the season, last season, and what we want to do this year, and that's go out and try to win another championship."[5]

As good as 2006 was for Johnson, 2007 was the year when NASCAR fans began considering Johnson as the best driver on the circuit.

Johnson won 10 races, becoming the first driver since Jeff Gordon in 1998 to hit double-digits in wins. Johnson's previous best was eight victories in 2004. For the second year in a row, he had 24 top-ten finishes. Even better, his top-five finishes jumped from thirteen in both 2005 and 2006 to twenty in 2007.

All that success pales in comparison, however, to the finish that Johnson displayed in the Chase for the Nextel Cup.

Johnson trailed Hendrick Motorsports teammate Gordon by nine points with three races to go in the Chase. Johnson, however, was driving with a surge of momentum. He had just won the previous two races at Martinsville and Atlanta to close the gap.

When Johnson won for the third week in a row at Texas and Gordon finished seventh, Johnson found himself with a 30-point lead with two races left. Johnson made it four victories in a row at Phoenix, with Gordon struggling to a tenth-place finish. The last person to win four races in a row? Gordon, in 1998.

Johnson had all but clinched the Nextel Cup title. All he needed to do was finish in eighteenth place or better in the finale at Homestead, Fla. He was steady in seventh at Homestead, and had his second consecutive Cup championship in hand.

Talk was already turning to Johnson replacing Gordon as the top driver in NASCAR.

"We're in elite company winning two championships, winning back to back championships is something I'm very, very proud of," Johnson said. "The good thing, I feel, is we're just really hitting our stride. I think we have a lot of good years ahead of us, and we'll be fighting for more championships and certainly winning more races as years go by. Hopefully we can be a three-time champion in the near future."[6]

**Jimmie Johnson celebrates after clinching his second straight Nextel Cup title in 2007.**

# CAREER STATISTICS

| Year | Rank | Starts | Wins | Poles |
|------|------|--------|------|-------|
| 2007 | 1 | 36 | 10 | 4 |
| 2006 | 1 | 36 | 5 | 1 |
| 2005 | 5 | 36 | 4 | 1 |
| 2004 | 2 | 36 | 8 | 1 |
| 2003 | 2 | 36 | 3 | 2 |
| 2002 | 5 | 36 | 3 | 4 |
| 2001 | 52 | 3 | 0 | 0 |

| Top 5 | Top 10 | Earnings | Points |
|---|---|---|---|
| 20 | 24 | $7,646,420 | 6,723 |
| 13 | 24 | $8,909,140 | 6,475 |
| 13 | 22 | $6,796,660 | 6,406 |
| 20 | 23 | $5,692,620 | 6,498 |
| 14 | 20 | $5,517,850 | 4,932 |
| 6 | 21 | $2,847,700 | 4,600 |
| 0 | 0 | $122,320 | 210 |

# CAREER ACHIEVEMENTS

2006        Won Nextel Cup
            championship; won the
            Daytona 500 and Brickyard
            400 in same season; tied
            for best start in NASCAR
            history with two wins
            and a second-place
            finish in his first three
            races; and voted NASCAR
            Driver of the Year.

2004        Topped all drivers
            with eight victories.

2002        Became first rookie to
            sweep both races at one
            track (Dover, California)
            and became first rookie
            to lead the Winston
            Cup point standings.

# FOR MORE INFORMATION

## ON THE WEB

**The Lowe's team racing site:**
www.lowesracing.com

**Jimmie Johnson's fan site:**
www.jimmiejohnson.net

**The Jimmie Johnson Foundation's site:**
www.jimmiejohnsonfoundation.org

## FURTHER READING

Gordon, Jeff, with Steve Eubanks. *Jeff Gordon: Racing Back to the Front.* New York: Atria Books, 2003.

LeMasters, Ron Jr. *Jimmie Johnson: A Desert Rat's Race to NASCAR Stardom.* St. Paul, Minn.: MBI Publishing, 2004.

# GLOSSARY

**American Speed Association**—The sanctioning body of motor sports in the United States from 1968 to 2004.

**Busch series**—A NASCAR circuit featuring slightly lighter and less powerful cars with events generally run the day before Nextel Cup races.

**caution flag (yellow flag)**—Requires drivers to slow down due to hazards on the track.

**crew chief**—The manager of a race team who oversees the mechanics of the car and the crew and is responsible for its performance on race day.

**driver**—The team member behind the wheel of the car on race day.

**fabricator**—Person who assembles parts or sections of a racecar.

**lap**—One trip around a track.

**NASCAR**—The National Association for Stock Car Auto Racing, which governs the Nextel Cup, formerly the Winston Cup series.

**Nextel Cup**—The championship won by earning the most points in a NASCAR season. Formerly known as the Winston Cup.

**pit stop**—Leaving the race track for service.

**pole position**—Earned in the qualifying race, the spot at the front of the grid to begin an event.

**Rookie of the Year**—The award given to the first-year NASCAR driver with the best fifteen finishes.

**sponsor**—The corporate entities that pay to have their logos and identities associated with particular race teams.

**stock car**—An automobile modified for racing used in NASCAR competition.

**team**—All employees and staff of an organization assigned to a particular car.

**Victory Lane**—A section of the track infield in which the winning car and team celebrate.

# CHAPTER NOTES

## CHAPTER 1. SILENCING THE CRITICS

1. Nate Ryan, "Johnson Wraps Up Nextel Cup Championship," *USA Today*, November 20, 2006, <www.usatoday.com/sports/motor/nascar/2006-11-19-homestead_x.htm> (February 2, 2007).

2. Mike Mulhern, "Johnson Wins 2006 NASCAR Championship," November 19, 2006, <http://www.timesdispatch.com/servlet/Satellite?pagename=Common%2FMGArticle%2FP> (February 2, 2007).

3. Nate Ryan, "Johnson Wraps Up Nextel Cup Championship," *USA Today*, November 20, 2006, <www.usatoday.com/sports/motor/nascar/2006-11-19-homestead_x.htm> (February 2, 2007).

4. Ibid.

5. Ibid.

## CHAPTER 2. DRIVING TOWARD A DREAM

1. Ron LeMasters Jr., *Jimmie Johnson: A Desert Rat's Race to NASCAR Stardom*, St. Paul, Minn.: Motorbooks International, 2004, p. 7.

2. Ibid., p. 10.

3. Ron LeMasters, Jr., "Off Road and on Track," *Stock Car Racing Magazine*, December 1999.

4. Ibid.

## CHAPTER 3. LEARNING THE ROPES

1. Ron LeMasters, Jr., "Off Road and on Track," *Stock Car Racing Magazine*, December 1999.

2. Ibid.

3. Ibid.

4. Bob Myers, "From The Desert to Daytona," *Circle Track*, May 2002.

5. Ron LeMasters, Jr., "Off Road and on Track," *Stock Car Racing Magazine*, December 1999.

## CHAPTER 4. RISING TO THE TOP

1. Bob Myers, "From The Desert to Daytona," *Circle Track*, May 2002.

2. Bob Myers, "From The Desert to Daytona," *Circle Track*, May 2002.

3. Ibid.

4. Johnson, Jimmie, "Driver's Seat," *Stock Car Racing Magazine*, March 2001.

## CHAPTER 5. A ROOKIE RUN FOR THE CUP

1. Press release, National Association for Stock Car Racing (NASCAR), May 1, 2003.

2. Jeff Gordon with Steve Eubanks, *Jeff Gordon: Racing Back to the Front*, New York: Atria Books, 2003, p. 216.

3. Larry Cothren, "Cool, Confident and Cashing In," *Stock Car Racing Magazine*, October 2002.

4. Geoff Shaw, "Golden Opportunity," *Scenedaily.com*, July 15, 2002, <www.scenedaily.com/stories/2002/07/15/scene_story2.html> (February 1, 2007).

5. Scoop Malinowski, "Red-Hot NASCAR Driver Jimmie Johnson," *The Biofile*, May 29, 2003, <www.thebiofile.com/articles/stories/56216390.php> (February 2, 2007).

6. *Stock Car Racing Magazine*, "People's Choice Awards' Biggest Surprise in 2002: Jimmie Johnson," November 2002.

## CHAPTER 6. GROWING INTO HIS ROLE

1. LeMasters, Jr., Ron. *Jimmie Johnson: A Desert Rat's Race to NASCAR Stardom*, Motorbooks International, St. Paul, Minn., 2004. p. 109.
2. Ron LeMasters Jr., *Jimmie Johnson: A Desert Rat's Race to NASCAR Stardom*, St. Paul, Minn.: Motorbooks International, 2004, p. 57.
3. Monte Dutton, "Johnson just goes about his business," *Gaston Gazette*, July 26, 2004.
4. Jimmie Johnson press conference, June 7, 2002.
5. Ron LeMasters Jr., *Jimmie Johnson: A Desert Rat's Race to NASCAR Stardom*, St. Paul, Minn.: Motorbooks International, 2004, p. 63.
6. Jason Mitchell, "The Stock Car Interview," *Stock Car Racing Magazine*, September 2003.
7. Ibid.

## CHAPTER 7. TRAGEDY AND CONTROVERSY

1. Marty Smith, "Conversation: Jimmie Johnson," *Nascar.com*, November 17, 2004, <http://nascar.com/2004/news/features/conversation/11/17/jjohnson_convo/index.html> (February 2, 2007).
2. Ibid.
3. Marty Smith, "Conversation: Jimmie Johnson," *Nascar.com*, January 18, 2005, <http://nascar.com/2005/news/features/conversation/1/18/jjohnson_convo/index.html> (February 2, 2007).
4. Ibid.
5. Mike Hembree, "Turn Four: Multiple wrecks litter track," *Scenedaily.com*, April 11, 2005, <http://jimmie_johnson.scenedaily.com/stories/2005/04/11/nextel_coverage5.html> (February 13, 2007).
6. Jim Utter, "Stewart, Johnson add another verse as NASCAR's discordant due du jour," *Thatsracin.com*, April 24, 2005, <http://thatsracin.com/mld/thatsracin/11479029.htm> (February 13, 2007).
7. Monte Dutton, "Darlington's not a bad place for Johnson to put it all behind him," *Gaston Gazette*, May 6, 2005.
8. Pockrass, Bob, "Johnson Shrugs off 'Idiot' Label from Junior," *scenedaily.com*, May 16, 2005, http://www.scenedaily.com/stories/2005/05/16/scene_circuit1.html (March 12, 2007).

## CHAPTER 8. STRUGGLES IN 2005

1. Reilly P. Brennan, "Jimmie Johnson Wins Coca Cola 600," *Motorsports Center*, May 30, 2005, <www.motorsportscenter.com/printer_588.shtml> (February 2, 2007).

2. Smithson, Ryan, "YIR: Jimmie Johnson," *nascar.com*, December 17, 2005, http://www.nascar.com/2005/news/headlines/cup/12/17/jjohnson/yir/index.html (March 12, 2007).

3. Ibid.

4. Corey Deitz, "NASCAR's Jimmie Johnson to Join XM Satellite Radio for Weekly Show," October 28, 2005, <http://radioabout.com/od/xmsatelliteradioprograms/a/aa102805a.htm> (February 2, 2007).

5. Marty Smith, "Conversation: Jimmie Johnson," *Nascar.com*, January 18, 2005, <http://nascar.com/2005/news/features/conversation/1/18/jjohnson_convo/index.html> (February 2, 2007).

## CHAPTER 9. AN UP-AND-DOWN SEASON

1. "2006 Daytona 500 Winner Jimmie Johnson Post Race Interview", *The Auto Channel*, February 19, 2006, http://www.theautochannel.com/news/2006/02/20/211067.html (March 12, 2007).

2. Ibid.

3. Ibid.

4. Bruce, Martin, "Johnson wins NASCAR Allstate 400 at the Brickyard," *USA Today*, August 6, 2006, http:ca.sports.yahoo.com/nascar/news?slug: nascar21&prov=st&type=lgns (March 12, 2007).

5. Ibid.

6. Ibid.

7. Bob Pockrass, "Johnson says everything is fine with Vickers," *Scenedaily.com*, October 14, 2006, <http://jimmie_johnson.scenedaily.com/stories/2006/10/09/scene_daily315.html> (February 2, 2007).

# CHAPTER 10. CROWNED A CHAMPION

1. "Jimmie Johnson Wins at Martinsville," *GM Racing Communications*, October 23, 2006, <http://www.catchfence.com/press/102306b.html> (February 2, 2007).

2. Harris, Mike, "Stewart Wins but Johnson Leads," *Associated Press*, November 6, 2006, http://www.boston.com/sports/other_sports/autoracing/articles/2006/11/06/stewart_wins_but_Johnson_leads/ (March 12, 2007).

3. Mike Mulhern, "Johnson Wins 2006 NASCAR Championship," November 19, 2006, <http://www.timesdispatch.com/servlet/Satellite?pagename=Common%2FMGArticle%2FP> (February 2, 2007).

4. "Jimmie and Chandra announce charitable foundation", *Lowe's Racing*, February 11, 2006, http://www.lowesracing.com/articles/20060211/705308.html (March 12, 2007).

5. "Jimmie Johnson Looks for Repeat," January 9, 2007, <http://www.thatsracin.com/mld/thatsracin/16421403.htm> (February 2, 2007).

6. Duane Cross, "Johnson dominant despite DNFs and point deductions," *nascar.com*, November 21, 2007, <http://www.nascar.com/2007/news/headlines/cup/11/21/jjohnson.how.he.won/index.html> (November 21, 2007)

# INDEX

FEB 2009

NO LONGER PROPERTY
OF HAWORTH
MUNICIPAL LIBRARY

HAWORTH PUBLIC LIBRARY, NJ

3 9137 09024175 8